Contents

Puberty: what's it all about?

There was a time when most blokes had to do tough, sweaty, dangerous jobs, which you can still do today if you choose to, but remember that men are also dancers, chefs, musicians — anything. You can be whatever you want to be, and it all starts when you grow from being a boy...

On the day you were born, you needed all the help you could get from adults to help you survive. Your brain was like a sponge, ready to soak up as much information as a super-computer! During your first year, you probably got 25 centimetres taller and three times heavier.

There was so much going on in your world that, by your third birthday, your brain would have been working overtime.

Now, you're reaching the time of your life known as puberty – the time when your brain and body are getting ready for your exciting future.

Did you know?

Your brain has stayed twice as active as an adult's ever since you were born! Result!

4

Q: What's the point of puberty?

A: Simple: it's to get you ready for your adult life. Puberty makes your body bigger, stronger and fertile, which means that you'll be able to become a father, if you wish, when the time is right. It's also the time when your brain functions begin to change, allowing you to think in different ways and start being independent. By the end of puberty, you will no longer be dependent on anyone else for survival.

Head start

Puberty often starts in girls before it starts in boys (irritating!), so the girls in your class may well be taller than you. But you'll soon catch up — and then overtake them. Yes!

Important point

Before you go any further, remember that puberty is different for everyone! There are no set rules, so what happens to your best mate when he is 12 years old may not happen to you until 14 or even older. There is nothing wrong if this happens – OK?

Essential stuff

Hormones are natural chemicals produced by your brain and then pumped around your body to make everything change. This is essential stuff for puberty.

First...

A hormone leaves your brain and zooms to your pituitary gland – that's a pea-sized gland sitting at the base of your brain – where it kick-starts the production of two more hormones.

and then...

These two hormones pump through your body to your reproductive system, where they create another hormone called testosterone. Testosterone is what's going to turn your boy's body into a man's one – grrr!

Boobs for boys

You may notice swelling or tenderness around one or both nipples at some stage. It's only temporary and may only last a few months. It's quite normal, and you're NOT turning into a woman. It's just your hormones going a bit nuts!

The same but different

Boys and girls all have pretty much the same hormones as each other, but they just do different things.

The five stages of puberty

Remember the ages here are all approximate and everyone starts puberty at different times. Some boys zoom through it and others take their time!

Stage 1 (from 9 to 12 years old). There's not much going on for anyone to see outside, but inside your hormones are being created and are starting to make your testicles mature. At the end of Stage 1, you may find you are suddenly getting much taller.

Stage 2 (from 9 to 15 years old). Your testicles and scrotum will gradually be getting larger, although your penis won't change much. You may begin to get some fine hair at the base of your penis. You're still getting taller and may be getting heavier.

Stage 3 (from 11 to 16 years old). You'll grow more pubic hair, and your testicles and scrotum will continue to get bigger. Although your penis is probably longer, it won't be any thicker. You'll also be growing even taller, your face may become broader and your voice will start to deepen.

Stage 4 (from 11 to 17 years old). Beneath your pubic hair, your testicles and scrotum are still growing, and your penis will get longer and thicker when it's not erect. You may ejaculate sperm for the first time. Your skin will become oilier and probably a bit spotty. Hair will appear under your arms and on your top lip and chin.

Stage 5 (from 14 to 18 years old). You'll be nearing your full height, and your shoulders will be broader. Your genitals and pubic hair will look more like a man's, and you'll have more hair on your face and body. You may well be shaving regularly.

Your bonkers brain

At the moment, your brain is only about 80 per cent developed. A computer geek might say that all the parts are there, they are just not fully wired up yet. When you hit puberty, your brain will fast-forward to its final size and capacity. It's a work in progress — and what progress your brain is going to make over the next few years!

With so much going on in your head during puberty, you may find some things completely baffle you. Getting the 'wiring' sorted out in your brain can take time, plus if you are growing fast, you can look and feel confused and clumsy. If that's the case, hang in there, things soon sort themselves out. By the end of puberty, you'll find that your brain has organized itself. It will have worked out the way you think and reason, and your decision-making skills will be complete. Other bits of your brain will be coping with your emotions and feelings.

Did you know?

Around the age of 16 is the best time to absorb new things. It's a great time to learn stuff – especially languages and music!

Time to Snooze

Because of all that brain and body activity during puberty, you need more sleep! In fact, you need about nine and a half hours of sleep each night.

Q&A

Q: Why is everything so weird? One minute I feel OK, but the next I'm so angry I feel I could explode! What's wrong?

A: Nothing's wrong. With so much growth going on, your emotions can be all over the place. If you liked something before, you probably feel passionate about it now. If you didn't like something once, you might positively despise it these days. Instead of just feeling sad, you might feel like the world is coming to an end. Trust us – it's not. That's what it's like being a teenager. Try to relax. Soon, everything will become less intense again. And remember, it's great to talk about things that are worrying you, with older brothers or lads, your dad, uncles, granddad, youth workers, sports coach or teachers – anyone you feel comfortable with.

Important point!

Your teen brain is more vulnerable than an adult one. This means the dangerous side-effects of alcohol and other drugs could have much more impact and long-term consequences. It's best to stay well clear of things like that!

Skin deep

Your skin is made up of three layers. The epidermis is the outer layer that you can see. Below that is the dermis where the nerve endings, sweat and oil glands, and blood vessels lie. Lower than the dermis lie the inner layers, where hair begins to grow. It is mostly made of fat.

blood vessel

epidermis

hair

sebaceous gland

sweat gland

Did you know?

Your skin is actually an organ! Not only that, it is the biggest organ you have because it covers your entire body.

How does skin work?

Firstly, it's a thick layer that prevents pollution from entering your body. Every day, you shed dead skin cells when you wash or simply by moving about. Your skin is constantly making new cells. But it uses a protein called keratin from the dead skin cells to make your skin waterproof.

Secondly, your skin regulates your body temperature. When it's hot, the sweat glands produce moisture to cool you down. When it's cold, the lower layer of your skin provides insulation.

Thirdly, a layer of fat protects you against bumps and knocks and acts as a bit of a shock absorber if you fall.

Sweat it out

Your skin is covered in little glands. If you want the fancy title, they are called sebaceous glands. There are loads of them on your forehead, nose, cheeks and chin. Puberty hormones make these glands go berserk. Suddenly your face becomes oily, and this oil can block the pores in your skin, causing spots. You may also notice that your skin goes from being baby smooth to feeling a bit rougher as you get older.

Get the message

There are receptors in the skin that respond to temperature, touch and pain. They send messages and signals straight to your brain! So, next time you hurt yourself, remember to say, "Oh good, my skin receptors are working really well"... er, if you can!

A bit of a stretch

Because of a rapid increase in your height and width, you might find that you get red stretch marks on the skin of your back, buttocks and thighs. These will fade, becoming pale and less noticeable as you get older. Many lads don't worry about these but if it concerns you, you may find that rubbing in some special skin lotions, available from a chemist, will make the marks less visible.

Keep it clean

With all that oil erupting on your face, it's essential to clean your face twice every day:

★ Use a gentle cleanser especially made for teenage skin. You can get ones that lather up for washing your face and neck before rinsing off with a clean flannel and lots of warm water.

★ Or you may prefer to use a cotton wool ball soaked in a liquid cleanser. Wipe it over your face and neck. You don't need to rinse off these sorts of cleansers. And remember, always read (and follow!) the instructions.

★ Whatever type of cleanser you prefer, always make sure that you clean all of your face, including under your fringe, behind your ears and your neck.

Zits are the pits!

When you get a spot, it can make you feel really down and a bit sensitive. So if you feel like teasing a lad (or girl) about their spots, remember, it could be your turn next!

Join the dots

One of the joys of puberty (not) is spots. They are caused by your pores getting clogged up by oily sebum. You're not alone. At least 90% of teenagers get spots at some stage in puberty. It's not a good idea to pick or squeeze spots but, OK, everyone does – just make sure your hands and nails are clean before going anywhere near that tempting zit. You could be squeezing bacteria into an open wound – not a great move.

Blackheads can be yellowish or black in colour. They look like bumps on your skin and may appear slightly pitted. The blocked sebum can appear black because it has reacted with the air.

Whiteheads are similar to blackheads but haven't changed colour. This is because the pore isn't open and the sebum has not been exposed to the air.

Acne is an angry inflammation of the skin, usually a mixture of blackheads, whiteheads and other types of spots – nice! It can be sensitive and itchy, but try to resist the urge to pick at acne. This could make it worse or even cause permanent scarring. If your acne is really bad, speak to a doctor or pharmacist.

Freckles are little brown spots on the skin caused by the sun. Everyone has pigment-producing cells in their skin called melanocytes. When the melanocytes are exposed to the sun, they make freckles on your face and body. If someone in your family has freckles or you have pale skin, you are more likely to have them. Using sun protection and keeping out of harsh sunlight will help prevent freckles.

Hairy bits and pieces

When puberty starts, it can seem as though you're covered in hair! It may seem annoying at times, but body hair is also important.

Hair protects your skin from germs, cushions the sensitive parts of your body and helps you to stay warm. Your body also uses the scent of your hair as a way to attract a mate, via naturally occurring chemicals called pheromones. This smell attracts others to you – dating made easy! But don't forget that there's a difference between the pheromones and unwashed socks – or armpits!

Q&A

Q: It's so embarrassing when I get changed for PE. I've got no hairs on my legs, but some other lads, well, you could almost plait their leg hairs. What's wrong with me?

A: Don't worry. Because puberty is different for everyone, hair grows at different times. And some men don't end up as hairy as others. The good news is, lots of men prefer to have a smooth body – and some girls like their blokes that way, too!

Hairy changes

Between the ages of 10 and 17, the hair you already have will start growing thicker, and new hair will appear. There is no 'right' age for this to happen. Every boy is different. Your body hair will continue to get thicker as you grow older.

Eyebrows get thicker and darker.

Hair will start to grow on your upper lip and chin.

Hair will grow under your armpits.

You may get hair growing on your back and buttocks in your later teens.

Some boys get hairs on the back of their hands.

Your legs will grow hair. Some boys have more hair below their knees than on their thighs; other boys are equally hairy the entire length of their legs.

A close shave

Q: I seem to have more facial hair than my mates and I feel embarrassed to have a moustache. What can I do about it?

A: It's more than likely your mates wish they were growing facial hair, too! If you don't like having facial hair, there's nothing for it other than to shave it off. Why not ask an older guy for some help?

Shaving rules!

★ Always use your own razor. Don't share with anyone else.

★ Never shave without covering the bits you are planning to shave with a shaving foam or gel.

★ Shave downwards, in the direction the hair grows, using long and even strokes.

★ Rinse your razor with water every second stroke to keep it from getting clogged with hair.

★ Shave cheeks and chin first, then upper lip. Curl your lip over your top teeth if it helps.

★ Use a styptic pencil, available from the chemist, if you get any cuts.

★ Wash off any excess shaving foam on your face with warm water.

★ Thoroughly clean and wash the razor before and after use.

★ Avoid after-shave on your face. It can irritate your skin.

★ Make sure the razor blades are sharp and replaced regularly.

Electrifying!

Electric razors can be harsh on younger skin and are more expensive than manual razors. Try using a disposable razor at first as it is a cheaper way of trying out different razors until you find the one you prefer.

The buzz of the fuzz or the shmooze of the smooth?

Some blokes prefer to have a hair-free chest and back to show off their muscles, but others think it's more 'manly' to have a hairy handful. Hairy or smooth – it's all a matter of personal preference. If you prefer to be a smoothie, shaving your chest will be time-consuming, and the hair will start to grow back almost immediately, and shaving your own back is near impossible! This hair is best removed by waxing, which means that hot wax is spread on your hairy bits and then ripped off with cloth strips.

Ouch!

Make no mistake, waxing off your body hair can hurt! It's also difficult to wax yourself so it's best to get it done by a professional.

Bad hair days

Some older men may not understand that some boys like to use hair products or straighteners, or even different styles and hair colours – in their day it was just 'short back and sides'. But nowadays, boys can style their hair to make them feel or look great!

Top tip

Make sure you rinse your hair properly after shampooing. If you leave soapy suds on the hair, it will make it look dull as it leaves a coating on the hair which can look like dandruff.

It's a wash-out

As the sebaceous glands on your scalp will be working overtime during puberty, producing more sebum and making your hair greasier than before, you may want to wash your hair every day. If you do, make sure you use a mild shampoo. Stronger shampoo has a lot of anti-grease astringents that can be harsh on your hair and irritate your scalp.

Be productive

If you use a lot of products, such as hair gel and styling mousse, make sure you wash them off thoroughly when you next shampoo, or you'll get a build up of gunk on your hair and scalp.

A common problem

Dandruff is flakes of dead skin from your scalp. Resist the urge to itch your scalp and use a gentle dandruff shampoo. Dandruff is not contagious.

Nit wits

Most people get head lice at some stage in their life (even teachers!). If you've got younger brothers and sisters, you might find you get them, too. Lice grip your hair and are virtually invisible to the naked eye. They feed on your scalp by biting and sucking your blood like mini vampires. Then they lay their sticky white eggs (nits) in your hair. The only certain way to clear yourself of lice is to use a special shampoo or lotion from the chemist and to follow the instructions carefully.

Nit pick

It's a myth that only people with dirty hair get lice and nits! In fact, they'll leap onto anyone's scalp if they are given the chance.

19

Where there's a willy, there's a way!

Every bloke has a penis. They come in a variety of shapes and sizes and get called lots of different names. Most importantly, you may be beginning to notice some changes in yours lately.

Well, what's it for?

A penis has two basic functions:
1. To let you get rid of urine.
2. For reproductive purposes – in other words, for passing sperm into a woman. Sperm are 'ejaculated': this is when white sticky stuff called semen shoots out from the small hole at the end of your penis.

shaft

foreskin

scrotum

Sizing it up

Some boys worry that their penis is too small. Well, no two are the same. Penises come in all shapes and sizes; no one's is completely straight, and a larger penis is not necessarily a better penis. Size does not matter. Got it? Good!

Don't get hung up

If you think your penis is too small, it almost certainly isn't, and it won't stop growing until you are 18 – or maybe even as old as 21! Penises are always smaller in cold water and weather. And don't forget either that a large flaccid (soft) penis may not get much bigger when it becomes erect – and a smaller penis can nearly double in size when it's erect!

Baby talk

Basically, when a man ejaculates during sex, semen is passed from the penis into the woman's vagina. The sperm in the semen then swim to the woman's womb (or uterus), looking for an egg to fertilize. If a sperm and an egg merge together, the woman will become pregnant. However, aside from all that, there's lots of emotional stuff involved with sex that's well worth mentioning. Sex is a BIG DEAL, and should only ever happen between two people who are ready both emotionally and physically. No one should have sex because:

★ Other people boast they are doing it.
★ A person thinks think it will make someone fancy them.
★ A person manages to talk someone into doing it.
★ A person thinks it will make them mature.

Contraception

A man and woman can have sex without the woman getting pregnant by using contraception. Some methods of contraception are also used to prevent people catching nasty diseases (known as STIs) from each other during sex.

Most importantly

If anyone has ever done anything physical to you that makes you feel uncomfortable or that you don't like, it's very important that you tell an adult you trust, such as a teacher.

Under pressure

There can be a big pressure on boys to boast about sex, which is daft and disrespectful (imagine if it was your sister a boy was talking about!). Most people don't have sex until they are over 16, so there's absolutely no rush.

Erections – the hard facts

An erection means that you are aroused. Extra blood flows into your penis making it grow longer and harder. You may find that during puberty, you get erections a lot, and often at embarrassing moments! It might be simply because you've walked past a group of girls or it might just happen for no apparent reason at all. If you're worried someone will notice, you could drop your bag or school books down in front of you. Some boys also find that wearing loose trousers helps cover things up. And remember: most boys of your age have the same problem.

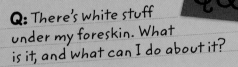

Q&A

Q: There's white stuff under my foreskin. What is it, and what can I do about it?

A: It's perfectly normal and it's called smegma. It's there to keep your foreskin lubricated. Clean behind your foreskin every day, so the smegma doesn't start to smell or make you itch.

Q: How do I keep my penis and scrotum clean?

A: With routine washing every day in the bath or shower. If you have a foreskin, gently ease it back and swish it around with water. You're better off washing your penis with just water, and using a gentle soap or shower gel to clean around the rest of the genital area.

Foreskin for you

You are born with a foreskin covering the head of your penis. In some cultures or for medical reasons, the foreskin is removed (this is called circumcision). If you still have a foreskin, make sure you keep the area around the head of your penis clean to reduce the risk of infection. And remember that your penis will function completely normally whether it has a foreskin or not!

Things that go bump in the night

If you notice white or yellow bumps on the skin at the head of your penis, don't pick them! They are quite normal. They are called papules and they are usually nothing to worry about. But some bumps and spots can be a sign of infection – if you are worried, get them checked out by your doctor.

Ball boy

You may find that your testicles go hard and feel uncomfortable when you have an erection. This is normal and will go away when your penis goes soft.

Another REALLY important thing to remember is how painful and dangerous it is to get hit in the testicles or hit someone else there. So avoid it at all costs!

It's also a good idea to get used to checking your testicles in the shower or bath. They are not perfectly round and smooth, but if you notice a lump or any pain or swelling, get it checked out by a doctor as soon as possible.

Safety in numbers

A man can produce as many as 30 million sperm every time he ejaculates.

Wet dreams

Some boys wake up and find the sheets are wet. It's not because they've wet themselves, it's because they have ejaculated in their sleep. As you get older, wet dreams will happen less frequently and then stop altogether. Some boys have a lot of wet dreams and some never have one at all!

Changing shape

Puberty is a time of such rapid change that it can seem like your body is different from one day to the next. Everyone worries about their body at some stage — that they're not tall, muscly or hairy enough. But remember that there's no one in the whole world as good at being you as you are!

Your arms and legs may suddenly grow longer and leaner and feel like they don't belong to you. So you might become quite clumsy, tripping over or knocking things over. Your shoulders may also start to broaden before you gain weight in proportion to them, so you might feel like a skinny weakling. Don't worry! Your muscles will soon start to bulk up naturally making your whole body look and feel much more normal!

Terrible teasers

Some people can be really thoughtless and tease lads about changes in their body shape. Add this to all those emotional changes we've talked about and it can be upsetting. If it does all get a bit much, remember there are adults you can trust to talk to — folks at home, teachers, youth workers. They are all on your side and will listen.

Growing pains

Over two or three years you may go through a massive growth spurt. It really can be possible for a shirt collar to do up one week and then not fit you the next! You might want to wait until you finish growing before you invest in those really expensive designer jeans!

24

Muscle bound

Don't get hung up on thinking you need to have a six-pack and perky pecs. It isn't natural for teenage boys to have such finely honed muscles. In fact, it's dangerous to get into a strict weight-lifting or body-building routine when you are still growing. Just keep generally fit by exercising or taking part in sport a few times a week and your muscles will develop naturally. And remember: almost every other boy your age has many of the same concerns.

Adam's apple

Everyone's got one – even girls! The proper name for it is the larynx. It's in your throat and it's where your voice comes from. It's also known as a voice box. During puberty, the larynx grows much more for boys. This is because your voice is going to get stronger and deeper. At some stage, your larynx will become more noticeable on your neck, sticking out a bit.

It's all in the name

Some people think an Adam's apple looks like something stuck in your throat, like a piece of apple – hence the name Adam's apple.

Q&A

Q: My voice keeps going squeaky! What's gone wrong?

Squeak!

A: Nothing! Your growing larynx is just geting used to its new size and sound. That's why one minute your voice seems higher and another it's deeper. It can be a bit of a pain sometimes – not knowing whether you'll growl or squeak when you open your mouth! Don't forget that half the humans on the planet will know how this feels, and it won't last forever.

25

Feeling fit

No one wants to look and feel like a couch potato. But then, no one wants to exercise so much that it becomes an unhealthy obsession either.

If you exercise and keep fit, you will:
★ Increase the 'happy hormones' in your body, giving you a feel-good factor – a kind of natural high.
★ Have more energy.
★ Have fun.
★ Make new friends.
★ Have brighter skin, hair and eyes.
★ Feel more toned and more confident in yourself.

If you stay a lounge lizard, you will:
★ Probably gain too much weight and have no muscle tone.
★ Have dull-looking skin, hair and eyes.
★ Get bored.
★ Have little energy.
★ Probably have low self-esteem.
★ Miss out on fun with your friends.
★ Not meet as many new friends.

Fantastic sports for fit teens

★ Team games, such as football, rugby, hockey, cricket, handball or basketball

★ Swimming

★ Skateboarding

★ Running

★ Cycling

★ Rowing

★ Tennis

★ Walking

★ Physically interactive computer games, such as Wii console games and dance games

★ Muscle-strengthening exercises such as squats, push-ups and crunches

Important point

Whatever exercise or sport you want to try out, get the right clothing and protective gear to make sure you don't hurt yourself – especially your teeth and genitals!

Have a go!

If you're interested in a new sport, you can find out where it's happening at a local community centre, gym or on the web. New people join sports clubs all the time, so they will be happy to welcome you in.

You are what you eat

Y ou start puberty with about 5 per cent body fat. By the end of puberty, you will have somewhere between 8 and 20 per cent, and it should stay this way throughout most of your adult life.

I'm starving!

Because you are growing fast and burning lots of energy doing it, you're probably feeling very hungry all the time! Make sure that you eat a mixture of healthy foods and treats, and keep active. If you have lunch at school, the dinners are usually healthy – if you make the right choices. These good habits will keep you fit for life!

Fact no. 1

Boys can consume between 3000 and 4000 calories a day if they are particularly active.

Fact no. 2

Boys gain about 1 to 1.5 kg every three months during puberty.

Vary it

A healthy diet is a varied one. Ideally, you should eat between three and five portions of fruits and vegetables a day. A glass of fruit juice or a smoothie can count as one portion! You also need to eat starchy, vitamin-rich foods such as bread, cereals, rice, pasta or potatoes. If you are a meat-eater, choose meats such as chicken and fish. Cut back on salty, fatty and sugary foods, such as chocolate, biscuits, crisps, butter, sausages and pies.

wake up and smell the breakfast

Don't be tempted to skip breakfast just so you can have another half-hour in bed. You might be bored of hearing this, but breakfast really is the most important meal of your day. Having had breakfast, you'll have more energy, be able to concentrate better at school and will be kept full until lunchtime. And your stomach won't rumble during morning classes – cringe! You could try talking to whoever does the food shopping at home – ask for nutritious food and offer to help with the preparation and cooking – or even the washing up! You might enjoy it and even become a famous master chef!

water-lot you've got!

Don't wait until you feel thirsty to take a drink because by that stage, your body is already beginning to dehydrate! Try to drink water instead of sugary and fizzy drinks. Water is better for your teeth, more refreshing, costs nothing if you take it from a tap and is calorie-free!

Weight worries

It's not just girls who worry about their weight. Boys can get hung up about dieting, too. Food is an essential part of living and one of the best things about it is enjoying eating it. If you eat too much and don't exercise or eat too little and exercise obsessively, you can get really ill. Anorexia nervosa and bulimia are two eating disorders that can develop during the teenage years. Sufferers can get tired easily, lose teeth and the hair on their head and have low self-esteem. If you are worried that you or someone you know may have an eating disorder, it's very important to speak to an adult about your concerns.

Eye-eye, Captain!

Your sight and your eyes are precious so you need to look after them. Make sure you:

★ Take regular exercise: eyes need oxygen to stay healthy, and keeping active will increase the oxygen supply to your body.

★ Don't spend too long in front of the TV or computer screen. The glare can strain your eyes.

★ Get enough sleep to rest your eyes.

★ Have regular eye tests: even if you don't think you have a problem, have a test as the optician can see inside your eyes, too, and check that everything is OK.

★ Wear glasses if you have been prescribed them: not doing so will make your eyes tired and sore.

★ Protect your eyes from the sun: wear sunglasses in summer and goggles if you go skiing.

Glasses: the long and short of it

If you are short-sighted, it means that you find it difficult to see things at a distance – like cinema screens or street signs. If you are long-sighted, it means you struggle to read books or text on screens. The great news is that, if you have to wear glasses, you will have loads of styles to choose from, and some girls might really fancy you (think of how intelligent you'll look!). If you do a lot of sport, select a pair of flexible frames and maybe get a band that attaches to your glasses and secures them to your head. You can also get prescription goggles if you do a lot of swimming.

Handle with care

To keep your specs in top-notch condition:

★ Keep them clean using the cloth in your case or use a special lens cleaner.
★ Don't put your glasses down and leave them resting on the lenses as they will get scratched.
★ Keep your glasses in their case when you aren't wearing them.

Make contact

Even though glasses are extremely cool, if you're fed up with them, you could consider contact lenses. You will need to ask your optician to see if contacts are right for you. They need to be kept in a special solution when not being worn, or they can damage your eyes. Many people wear disposable contact lenses, which are much easier to care for.

31

Top-notch gnashers

You need your teeth to eat and to communicate, so you don't want to have filled or dirty teeth. Keeping your teeth clean now will set you up for life!

Remember to:

★ Brush your teeth twice a day for about two minutes each time.

★ Brush in small circles, not across or up or down.

★ Use a fluoride toothpaste and a toothbrush that's right for your age.

★ Clean between your teeth with floss once a day, preferably before bedtime.

★ Change your toothbrush regularly. You'll know it needs changing when the bristles start to curl at the top.

All fizzled out

It's best to sip fizzy drinks and fruit juice through a straw, so the sugar doesn't coat your teeth as much. Also, don't brush your teeth straight after drinking sugary drinks as it can soften the enamel. It's better to wait about 30 minutes and rinse your mouth with water before brushing.

Mega molars

You'll have most of your adult teeth by the time you are 14 years old, but there will be some molars that wait until 17 or even older before erupting. These are your third molars and are most commonly known as wisdom teeth. Lots of people don't have enough space in their mouth for wisdom teeth, so dentists like to make regular checks on them.

Close contact!

If you do any kind of contact sport (such as hockey, cricket, football or rugby) always wear protection for your teeth. A gumshield can prevent broken teeth and damage to your gums. You can buy one quite cheaply at a sports shop and follow the instructions to make it fit your own mouth.

Brace yourself

Lots of teens wear braces because their teeth are crooked, over-crowded or don't bite together properly. Braces may have to be worn for a few months or up to three years. If you wear braces, always make sure you follow the correct advice about keeping your teeth and braces clean – there's no point having lovely, straight teeth just to let them decay, is there? No one is crazy about having a mouth full of metal, but it will be worth it in the end. Just think of that smile – or the trips to the dentist you'll avoid when you are older!

What a stinker!

Pongy breath can be caused by smoking, certain foods, not cleaning your teeth properly and, rarely, because of a medical disorder. Cleaning your teeth, gums and tongue regularly will usually keep smelly breath at bay. If it doesn't, speak to your dentist.

Clean up your act!

All day, every day, your skin is producing sebum, sweat and, at the same time, shedding dead skin cells. Bacteria, found in the air around us, join this mixture whether you like it or not and — ta-da! — your body starts to smell. Actually, in some boys some bits of their body start to smell stronger than others. This smell is known as body odour (BO for short).

You can keep the smell under control by:

★ Washing every day, preferably in the shower or bath.
★ Drying thoroughly everywhere after washing.
★ Hanging your towel up after you have used it and changing it every few days.

★ Using an anti-perspirant deodorant to stop your armpits from smelling.
★ Wearing a clean shirt every day.
★ Changing out of your school uniform when you get home each day. Hang the uniform up to air when you aren't wearing it.
★ Always showering after exercise and changing into fresh clothes afterwards.

Guess what?
You've got **3 MILLION** sweat glands all over your body. Everybody has!

Sniff it out!

If you suspect you have a bit of BO, don't wait for someone to tell you that you stink before you do something about it. Get into a routine of washing regularly and then you won't have to worry about it.

Deodor-don't

Lots of boys like to wear deodorant to make sure they smell good. But be warned: deodorant won't cover up the stink of sweat underneath. You need to wash before you spray it on. Also, make sure you wash regularly to rinse away the smell you sprayed on earlier. If you don't, the body spray itself will start to smell stale and it will also block pores, adding to the likelihood of BO.

Feet first

Feet are often the first things to grow when puberty kicks in. They may increase so rapidly in size that you'll outgrow new shoes in no time! Some boys find that their feet have reached their full size by 15 years old.

Q&A

Q: My feet really stink — even I can smell them! How can I stop them ponging?

A: There are a number of things you can do:
- ★ Wash your feet every day and dry them thoroughly.
- ★ Wear clean cotton socks daily.
- ★ Wear different socks for sport, and change out of them afterwards.
- ★ Don't wear trainers all the time. Alternate with leather or other well-ventilated shoes.
- ★ When you take your shoes off, leave them somewhere so they can air.
- ★ Keep toenails clean and short.
- ★ Go barefoot for at least some of the time at home.
- ★ Use scented insoles and foot powders available from chemists.

The big stink

Your feet are covered in sweat glands that contain salt and water, which are secreted out constantly. Imagine cramming those feet inside a pair of shoes for a day and mixing all that sweat with bacteria in your shoes and socks — it's a steamy thought, isn't it? And it's also a smelly one. Having smelly feet is technically called bromohydrosis. But it doesn't really matter what it's called, because it still honks.

Vile verrucas

Everyone's heard of verrucas but few people will admit to having one. It's a pity because verrucas are highly contagious. Officially they're known as plantar warts. Verrucas are warts that have been pushed to the surface of the skin on the sole of your foot by the weight of your body.

Changing rooms!

All that walking around barefoot in the changing rooms at school and the local swimming pool makes you vulnerable to verrucas. To avoid the infections that cause verrucas, you should try...

★ Not walking around barefoot while you change.

★ Standing on a towel when your socks are off.

★ Walking to the poolside in flip-flops or watersport shoes.

★ Wearing special swimming socks – these are available from sports shops, chemists and some swimming pools. You should also wear these if you have a verruca to stop anyone else catching it!

Your family and other animals

Pesky parents

Let's admit it: sometimes you take your parents (or whoever looks after you at home) for granted. They do pretty much everything for you. But they take something for granted, too: that they're in charge. Sometimes it can feel like your folks at home are trying to rule your life. The thing is, when they were your age, they used to feel just like you do. So talk to older people you can trust, not just about problems and worries, but about all the brilliant things in your life. They may not understand just how hard that computer game level really is, but they care for you and want the best for you. They might even let you have an extra 10 minutes on that noisy drum kit or guitar game if they know how much it means to you!

Stupid siblings

Your older brothers and sisters probably seem like they spend all their time pushing you around. And the younger ones? They drive you nuts being in your face all day and wanting you to play their baby games.

And then there's you...

You are getting older and you want to be treated like an adult. But on the other hand, sometimes you just can't cope with the responsibility people expect of you. You've got pressure at school. You want to spend time with your friends. And sometimes, you just want to sit at home and play video games or be spoiled rotten by your gran! One minute you are happy, the next minute you feel like stomping about in anger – and you don't even know why!

Let's take a minute to chill out. There are ways to cope with your family relationships. Try to remember:

★ There's no rush to grow up.
★ Don't keep your friends a secret from your parents – bring them back to the house to hang out.
★ If you want to be treated like an adult, then don't throw toddler tantrums.
★ Your parents love you a whole lot; they are not your enemies.
★ Talk to your parents about how you feel, and listen to their point of view.
★ Ask if you can have more privacy. If you share a bedroom, try to work out a way where you and your sibling can each have personal space.
★ Spend a little time with your family. If you never do, then you'll never be able to have any fun with them.

Mates and dates

Until now, girls have just been the same old kids in your class they've always been. But lately, some of them seem a bit more interesting. Possibly quite attractive. Quite funny. Quite fanciable...

Totally crushed

There's a girl at school that you can't stop thinking about, but you are too shy to speak to her. Or perhaps there's a dead cool sports teacher. You wish you were like him and dressed like him...

Welcome to the world of crushes. It's like having a minor obsession with someone – anyone! It could be a girl, a boy, a teacher, a celebrity – whoever it is, it's perfectly normal. When you've got a crush, the intense feelings might feel like they're taking over your life, but in time your feelings will die down.

Q&A

Q: Lately I've started to have feelings for another boy. Aren't I supposed to only like girls?

A: Loads of kids have same-sex crushes during puberty – they just might not admit it! Everyone has their own preferences for crushes – some boys like girls with black hair, some boys like girls with fair hair, and some boys like boys! If, when you are older, you still like people of your own sex, that's absolutely fine.

The thing about girls

You might think girls can be right stroppy! One day they might take a fancy to you and the next they completely ignore you! Just remember: girls your age are also going through puberty, so their feelings can be all over the place, too.

Best buds

When you start secondary school, you'll meet a whole bunch of new friends. But try not to drop your old ones. As you get older, your friendship circle will be made up of lots of different people.

The secret to having great friends is recognizing the ones that are good for you and those who aren't. Talk to someone you trust if you feel unhappy about a certain friendship.

FRIENDSHIPS SHOULD:
★ be fun.
★ make you feel good.
★ be reliable.

FRIENDSHIPS SHOULDN'T:
★ make you feel bad about yourself.
★ make you feel insecure.
★ be hard work.
★ tempt you into things that you feel unhappy about.

The trouble with drugs

As you grow up to become a teenager, you'll have all sorts of brilliant things to look forward to but there are also some things to avoid or be careful of. Other lads might encourage you to smoke cigarettes or take other drugs – how stupid is that? Drugs affect young, growing people even more than they do adults, and can lead to some really nasty consequences.

A drinking problem

The problem with alcohol (apart from it being illegal before the age of 18) is that it can make people do daft things. And sure, daft things can be funny sometimes, but not when they lead you to do something dangerous or violent. Alcohol in moderation might be OK for some adults, but this is a decision to make when you're older. Remember that they are your decisions; doing something just because you think other people are doing it or letting other people decide what happens to you is just plain crazy!

Cool school

*S*ome say that school days are the best of your life, but you might not agree with that right now. Even if you don't like all your subjects, and some of your teachers seem a bit odd, the fact is that you have to spend a lot of time at school, so you might as well do your best to enjoy it.

Q&A

Q: We do so many stupid subjects. I can't see the point — why should I bother?

A: It's understandable, but, the thing is, you need to get through your exams so you can go on to the next bit of your education and get a job. You'll find things really difficult if you don't have qualifications. When you're about to throw in the pencil, try to focus on the goal at the end, and think positive thoughts: "If I just push through and get a decent grade, then I can stop this subject and never have to do it ever again in my life!"

Q: I'm starting at a new school soon. How can I make sure I fit in?

A: Everyone is a bit nervous when starting at a new school. Just be yourself and make it clear you want to make friends. Don't try to big yourself up, thinking it will impress people. You'll soon trip yourself up with your fibs and end up losing friends. You don't have to change the way you dress or behave to get attention or to blend in with others. You'll soon find friends that like you for who you are.

Bullying boys

There's always someone who wants to be the loudest, funniest, most attention-grabbing person at school. And that's fine, as long as they don't go about it by making fun of someone else. Bullies don't just use their size or strength to scare people. They do it by excluding people, too – maybe by spreading rumours online or by gossiping, or by speaking to people in a way that makes them feel humiliated. Bullies don't just do it on their own: most of them have a gang behind them. The truth is, their leader is really a coward who is too scared to do the bullying on his or her own, and the gang is too scared to stand up to the leader.

It's not just boys...

Girls can be bullies, too! Not just to other girls either. Don't be embarrassed to tell your teacher if a girl is giving you a hard time.

Stand proud!

You can stand up to bullies by not letting them get away with it. Your school will have a policy about bullying – go and speak to the person who is in charge of it or a teacher you trust. And if you see someone else being bullied (even if it's someone you don't know or like) stand up for them anyway. No one need ever know that you told someone about it, and you may well save someone a whole heap of trouble!

Networking

I t's great chatting away to friends on your computer or mobile phone, but your parents just don't get it. When they were your age, they didn't have mobiles or social networking sites, so no wonder they don't understand why you're having so much fun.

Hanging on the telephone

Your phone is your lifeline to independence. Don't risk losing it!

Don't:
★ Spend too much credit.
★ Ignore your parents when they try to contact you.
★ Use your phone during school unless you have permission to.
★ Leave your phone in a stupid place or make it easy for someone to steal it.
★ Send rude texts or photos to anyone (even if it seems like a laugh at the time).
★ Forward any viral messages you receive.
★ Plug earphones into your ears when you're on a busy road, or somewhere else where you need your hearing.

Do:
★ Use your phone to keep in touch with your parents.
★ Keep it switched on when you are with your mates.
★ Keep it charged at all times.
★ Tell an adult if you are being hassled through your phone.
★ Delete any viral messages that other kids are spreading.
★ Only give your number to people you know and trust.
★ Keep aware when using your phone outside.
★ Take your phone out of your pocket before your clothes are washed!

Use your cyber sense

The Internet is a great ways to keep in touch, but it can be a tricky place to stay safe in. And the things you intend to say privately are really not private at all. Pay attention to these wise words:

★ Keep your password secret and change it every so often.

★ Keep your friendship groups to only the people you know 100 per cent – not just someone who seems friendly who you haven't met.

★ Only put up posts, photos and comments that won't embarrass or humiliate you or your friends (or even people you don't especially like).

★ Lock your profile so others can't meddle with it, and don't mess with other people's profiles.

★ Remember that teachers, colleges and even future employers may check social networking sites to see what you've been up to. What seemed funny last night might not seem so clever tomorrow.

★ Remember that even if you delete something you regret doing earlier, someone may already have saved it elsewhere. What you put on the Internet is there forever.

★ Don't let someone coax you into doing or saying something online that you feel uncomfortable about. Report cyber pests and bullies to site monitors.

Glossary

adolescence / adolescent The time in your life also known as puberty / someone who is going through puberty.

anorexia nervosa An eating disorder that leads someone to fear becoming overweight, resulting in excessive dieting and exercising, illness, and even death.

anus The hole in your bottom where solid waste comes out when you go to the toilet.

bulimia nervosa An eating disorder that leads someone to eat large amounts of food in short bursts, and then make themselves vomit afterwards. It can result in illness, and even death.

cervix The entrance to the womb at the top of the vagina.

contraception The general name for different ways to stop a woman becoming pregnant.

dandruff Flakes of dead skin from your scalp.

ejaculate/ejaculation The ejection or discharge of sperm from the penis.

follicle A tiny hole in your skin where a hair grows. You have many follicles.

gland A cell or organ that makes chemical substances and then releases them for the body to use or get rid of.

hormone A chemical substance made by a gland and then transported around the body.

keratin A protein found in the outer layer of skin which makes it waterproof; keratin is a protein also found in nails and hair.

perspiration A salty fluid released by the sweat glands of the skin; it is also called sweat.

pheromone A chemical substance secreted unnoticed by humans but which can affect the behaviour and reaction to others.

pituitary gland A gland attached to a stalk at the base of the brain, which releases hormones relating to skeletal growth and the reproductive system.

puberty The time in your life, also known as adolescence, when your body prepares itself for adulthood.

pubic hair Hair on the genital area.

scrotum The pouch of skin containing the testes, or testicles.

sebum The oily substance that acts as a lubricant for the hair and skin.

semen The thick whitish liquid containing sperm that is ejaculated from the penis.

smegma A whitish sebaceous substance that lubricates the foreskin.

sperm Male reproductive cells; also known as spermatozoa.

sweat A salty fluid released by the sweat glands of the skin.

testicles The two reproductive glands that produce sperm.

testosterone A hormone secreted by the testes.

vagina The tube that leads from the cervix of the womb to an outer opening, in between the urethra and anus.

womb A hollow organ lying within the abdomen of a woman, in which a baby grows.

Notes for parents and teachers

We talk to girls about puberty, especially periods, but we don't seem to talk to boys as much. These can be turbulent times for young people, their families and teachers, but research has shown the importance of establishing and maintaining relationships with boys from childhood into adulthood. It can feel daunting, but this book is designed to help boys (although their sisters might also find it interesting) through this transformation.

- Familiarize yourself with this book and learn when and how to describe the physical changes, adult emotions or themes in a way that a child can understand.

- Many boys find it hard to discuss their feelings, so you may prefer to leave him to read this book on his own, and then invite questions later.

- Don't try to give all the information at once. Offer small amounts and invite him to question you.

- Try talking in informal situations, such as on a walk, kicking a ball about or even watching TV.

- Taking an interest in his hobbies and praising him (rather than the nagging that some youngsters complain about) can make such a difference.

- Boys need positive male role models in their lives. Older cousins, uncles, youth workers and granddads are all potential role models – and boys often need to talk with someone just that bit further away from home.

- Teachers are incredibly important. Check that your school policy supports you teaching and answering questions. If it doesn't, find out what you can do to update it.

The boys in our care will mirror the ways that we treat them and treat each other. The personal relationships that we build with them can prepare them to deal with any difficult times they may face. They need and deserve a solid foundation of love and trust, based on honest, open communication.